The Life Cycle of a
Penguin

by Lisa Trumbauer

Consulting Editor: Gail Saunders-Smith, Ph.D.

Consultant: Brandie Smith, Assistant Director,
Conservation and Science
American Zoo and Aquarium Association
Silver Spring, Maryland

Pebble Books

an imprint of Capstone Press
Mankato, Minnesota

Pebble Books are published by Capstone Press
151 Good Counsel Drive, P.O. Box 669, Mankato, Minnesota 56002
http://www.capstone-press.com

1 2 3 4 5 6 08 07 06 05 04 03

Library of Congress Cataloging-in-Publication Data
Trumbauer, Lisa, 1963–
    The life cycle of a penguin / by Lisa Trumbauer.
    p. cm.—(Life cycles)
    Includes bibliographical references and index.
    Summary: Describes the physical characteristics, habits, and stages of
development of penguins.
    ISBN 0-7368-2090-6 (hardcover)
    1. Penguins—Life cycles—Juvenile literature. [1. Penguins.] I. Title. II. Life cycles
(Mankato, Minn.)
QL696.S473 T78 2004
589.47—dc21   2002154706

Note to Parents and Teachers

The Life Cycles series supports national science standards related
to life science. This book describes and illustrates the life cycle
of a king penguin. The life cycles of other penguin species differ
slightly. The images support early readers in understanding the
text. The repetition of words and phrases helps early readers
learn new words. This book also introduces early readers to
subject-specific vocabulary words, which are defined in the Words
to Know section. Early readers may need assistance to read some
words and to use the Table of Contents, Words to Know, Read
More, Internet Sites, and Index/Word List sections of the book.

Table of Contents

Photographs in this book show the life cycle of a king penguin.

egg

4

Egg

A penguin begins life as an egg. Both penguin parents take turns keeping the egg warm.

2 months

Chick

A chick hatches after
about two months.
Soft feathers called
down cover the chick.

The chick stands
on its parent's feet
to keep warm.

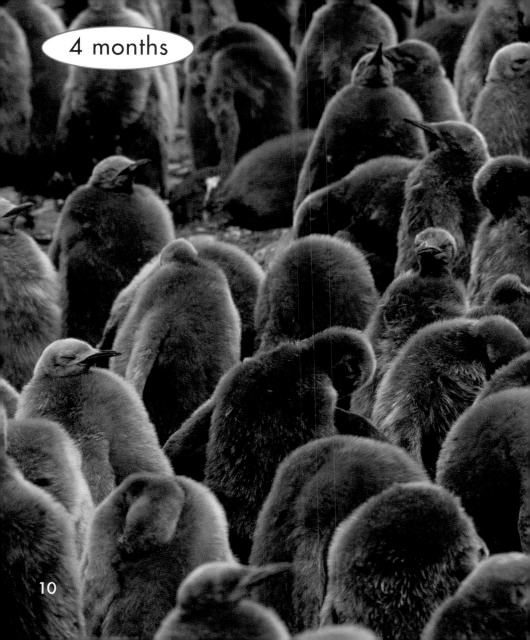

4 months

Young Penguin

The chick grows. It stands with other young penguins to stay warm.

The mother and father penguin feed the young penguin. They spit food into its mouth.

1 year

14

New feathers grow
on the young penguin.
Now the penguin
can swim.

5 years

Adult

The penguin becomes an adult. Penguins can live up to 20 years.

A male and female penguin mate.
The female penguin usually lays one egg.

chick

young penguin

egg

adult

The Life Cycle

The egg is the start
of a new life cycle.

Words to Know

adult—an animal that is able to mate

down—the soft feathers of a young bird; penguin chicks with down cannot swim until new feathers grow; down feathers are not waterproof.

feather—one of the light, fluffy parts that covers a bird's body; penguin's adult feathers are shiny and waterproof.

hatch—to break out of an egg

life cycle—the stages of life of an animal; the life cycle includes being born, growing up, having young, and dying; female penguins usually start to lay eggs when they are about five years old.

mate—to join together to produce young; some female penguins mate with the same male penguin each year.

CRead More

Reid, Keith. *Penguin: Habitats, Life Cycles, Food Chains, Threats.* Natural World. Austin, Texas: Raintree Steck-Vaughn, 2001.

Schafer, Kevin. *Penguins A-B-C.* Chanhassen, Minn.: NorthWord Press, 2002.

Swan, Erin Pembrey. *Penguins: From Emperors to Macaronis.* Animals in Order. New York: Franklin Watts, 2003.

CInternet Sites

Do you want to find out more about penguins? Let FactHound, our fact-finding hound dog, do the research for you.

Here's how:

1) Visit *http://www.facthound.com*

2) Type in the **Book ID** number: **0736820906**

3) Click on **FETCH IT**.

FactHound will fetch Internet sites picked by our editors just for you!

(Index/Word List

Word Count: 114
Early-Intervention Level: 12

Editorial Credits
Sarah L. Schuette, editor; Kia Adams, series designer; Jennifer Schonborn, interior
    designer; Enoch Peterson, production designer; Kelly Garvin, photo researcher;
    Karen Risch, product planning editor

Photo Credits
Joe McDonald, 1
Joe McDonald/Tom Stack & Associates, 6, 20 (top)
Sylvia Stevens, 8, 12
Visuals Unlimited/Joe McDonald, cover (adult), 4, 18, 20 (left); Elizabeth DeLanry,
    cover (chick); Beth Davidon, 10; Gerald & Buff Corsi, 14, 16, 20 (bottom, right)